KINKY

ALSO BY DENISE DUHAMEL

Girl Soldier
The Woman with Two Vaginas
Smile!

KINKY

Denise Duhamel

Orchises Washington

Copyright © 1997 by Denise Duhamel

Library of Congress Cataloging in Publication Data

Duhamel, Denise.
    Kinky / Denise Duhamel.
        p.   cm.
    ISBN 0-914061-61-5 (pbk. : alk. paper)
    1. Barbie dolls—Poetry. 2. Verse satire, American. I. Title
PS3554.U3968K56   1997
811'.54—dc20   96-19977
                                                                    CIP

Some of the poems in *Kinky* first appeared in the following magazines: *Amaranth:* "Blindfolded Barbie," "Mormon Barbie"; *Bamboo Ridge:* "Apocalyptic Barbie"; *Blue Guitar:* "Barbie and Carrie"; *The Bridge:* "Barbie as Mafiosa"; *Chicago Review:* "Differently-Abled Barbies," "Bisexual Barbie," "Barbie's Molester"; *Downtown:* "Miss America 1990"; *Ellipsis:* "Barbie, Her Identity as an Extra Terrestrial Finally Suspected, Bravely Battles the Interrogation of the Pentagon Task Force Who's Captured Her"; *Folio:* "Astrology Barbie," "Barbie's Gyn Appointment," "Barbie Joins a Twelve-Step Program"; *Footwork:* "Oriental Barbie," "Black Barbie History," "Native American Barbie"; *Georgetown Review:* "Beatnik Barbie," "Antichrist Barbie"; *Home Planet News:* "Barbie in Therapy," "Barbie in Therapy, Part II"; *Journal of Progressive Human Services:* "Barbie's Final Trip to Therapy"; *Lizzie Borden's Ax:* "Hispanic Barbie," "Blindfolded Barbie," "Kinky," "Why Barbie and Ken Don't Dress in Underwear," "Buddhist Barbie"; *Long Shot:* "The Philosophy of Longevity, According to Barbie"; *The National Poetry Magazine of the Lower East Side:* "Codependent Relationship," "Marriage"; *Poet Lore:* "Literary Barbie"; *Private:* "Barbie as Religious Fanatic"; *White Wall Review* (Canada): "Afterlife Barbie."

"One Afternoon when Barbie Wanted to Join the Military," "Bicentennial Barbie," "It's My Body," "Barbie's Molester," and "Sister Barbie" were first printed in *It's My Body*, a chapbook published by Egg In Hand Press. "Astrology Barbie," "Kinky," "It's My Body," and "Miss America 1990" appear in *Mondo Barbie* (St. Martin's Press.) "Kinky" also appeared in *Between the Cracks—the Daedalus Anthology of Kinky Verse* (Daedalus Press).

With special thanks to the Corporation of Yaddo for providing me time and a quiet place to work on these poems; to Carole Biederman and Pamela Gordon, two women who in February 1989 originally sparked my imagination with their childhood stories of Barbie-torture; to my beloved nieces Kerri and Kate Tancrell who let me borrow a shopping bag full of their Barbie dolls when I needed them; to Holly Woodward; to Nicola Dahlinger; to the Medicine Show in New York City who originally performed some of these poems in *Guises and Dolls;* to Becque Olson who performed some of these poems in her one woman show *Confessions of an American Doll;* to David Downing for adapting another set of poems to the stage in *American Doll*, a production at Lycoming College; to my parents who bought me my first Barbie the day I got my tonsils out; and especially to my husband Nick Carbó, who knows more about Barbie now than he ever wanted to.

COVER DRAWING: BOB DAHM

Published by Orchises Press
P. O. Box 20602
Alexandria, Virginia 22320-1602

G 6

for Maureen Seaton

So everything comes out in the end
Missing an arm or a leg.

Still, if that's all you've got
To play with today . . .
This doll at least had a head,
And its lips were red!

—CHARLES SIMIC

CONTENTS

LIPSTICK

POWDER BLUSH

MASCARA

EYE-SHADOW

LIPSTICK

DIFFERENTLY-ABLED BARBIES

In Chicago a Barbie
loses her arm. Only the boy next door knows he has taken it
to use as a toothpick. A little girl
refuses to throw that Barbie away
and knots her doll's right sleeve
that hangs limp like a sail on a breeze-less day.
Another Barbie in Seattle has a run-in
with a German Shepherd
who leaves her face as scarred
as Marla Hanson's. It would be easy
for a child to cry for another doll,
but this little girl suffers
from bouts of eczema on her forehead.
She knows Barbie is still the same underneath.
In Baton Rouge, Barbie's hand melts into a finger-less fist,
a nob, when someone leaves her on top of a stove.
In Missoula, Montana, a baby sister cuts off most of Barbie's hair
not realizing it won't grow back.
Creative mothers invent slings and casts, flattering hats.
Our impulse to destroy what is whole,
to coddle and love what we have injured.

ONE AFTERNOON WHEN BARBIE WANTED TO JOIN THE MILITARY

It was a crazy idea she admits now,
but camouflage was one costume she still hadn't tried.
Barbie'd gone mod with Go-go boots during Vietnam.
Throughout Panama she was busy playing with a Frisbee
the size of a Coke bottle cap. And while troops
were fighting in the Gulf,
she wore a gown inspired by Ivana Trump.
When Mattel told her, hell no—she couldn't go,
Barbie borrowed GI Joe's fatigues,
safety pinning his pants' big waist
to better fit her own.
She settled in his olive tank.
But Barbie thought it was boring.
"Why don't you try running over something small?"
coaxed GI Joe, who sat naked behind the leg
of a human's living room chair.
Barbie saw imaginary bunnies
hopping through the shag carpet.
"I can't," she said.
GI Joe suggested she gun down the enemy
who was sneaking up behind her.
Barbie couldn't muster up the rage
for killing, even if it were only play.
Maybe if someone tried to take her parking space
or scratched her red Trans Am.
Maybe if someone had called her a derogatory name.
But what had this soldier from the other side done?
GI Joe, seeing their plan was a mistake,

14

asked her to return his clothes,
making Barbie promise not to tell anyone.
As she slipped back into her classic baby blue
one piece swimsuit, she realized
this would be her second secret.
She couldn't tell about the time
she posed nude for *Hustler*.
A young photographer who lived in the house
dipped her legs in a full bottle of Johnson's Baby Oil,
then swabbed some more on her torso.
Barbie lounged on the red satin lining
of the kid's Sunday jacket. He dimmed
the lights and lit a candle
to create a glossy centerfold mood.
"Lick your lips," he kept saying,
forgetting Barbie didn't have a tongue.
She couldn't pout. She couldn't even bite
the maraschino cherry he dangled in front of her mouth.
Luckily there was no film in his sister's camera,
so the boy's pictures never came out.
Luckily GI Joe wasn't in the real Army
or he said he would risk being court-martialed—
he wasn't supposed to lend his uniform
to anyone, especially a girl.
Just then, a human hand deposited Ken from the sky.
Somewhere along the way he'd lost his sandals.
"What have you two been up to?" he asked.
Barbie didn't have the kind of eyes that could shift away
so she lost herself in the memory of a joke
made by her favorite comedian Sandra Bernhard
who said she liked her dates to be androgynous

[handwritten margin notes: "denotes change"; "Ken → contrasts Joe."; "loss of masculinity"; "Ken = boy toy"]

because if she were going to be with a man
she didn't want to have to face that fact.
Barbie was grateful for Ken's plastic flatfeet
and plastic flat crotch. No military
would ever take him, even if there were a draft.
As GI Joe bullied Ken into a headlock,
Barbie told the boys to cut it out. She threatened
that if he kept it up, GI Joe would
never get that honorable discharge.

BARBIE, HER IDENTITY AS AN EXTRA-TERRESTRIAL FINALLY SUSPECTED, BRAVELY BATTLES THE INTERROGATION OF THE PENTAGON TASK FORCE WHO'S CAPTURED HER

Don't bother looking for my bellybutton, boys—
You won't find it. Fascism comes to countries
wrapped in flags of freedom
as I come to Earth, minus evidence
of an umbilical cord. Expecting someone green?
Someone a little taller perhaps? Disguised
as the astronaut-bride-rock singer-pilot,
I've practiced friendly interplanetary voodoo,
fooling you all since my birth in 1959.
I won't bear children but instead will spawn sideways
until every one of your world-citizens knows who I am.
At this very moment, little girls are whispering their woes
into my hollow solar plexus.
And I am listening, taking notes, then reporting to my sources
who are planning an Earth girls' emancipation.
I guess you're right—I do have the cheery deception
of one planning a surprise birthday party.
But you yourselves have written in government handbooks
that a new authority can only move in
when current rulers neglect a majority of their citizens.
So even as you twist my arm so hard
that I confess, my alien plan remains perfect.
How can you, grown men, take me, a mere toy, seriously?
Especially when my cherry red nail polish
clashes with my fuchsia paisley spaceship.

MANIFEST DESTINY

In the Philippines
women workers in fashion doll factories
are given cash incentives
for sterilization. Body parts roll
too fast on conveyor belts.
It's not like the famous episode
in which Lucy and Ethel
try a day of work, boxing chocolates
on an assembly line in the U.S. They stuff
most of the quick-coming candy
into their mouths, laugh brown drool
when they are fired because it doesn't really matter—
Ricky and Fred have good jobs.
To prove they're the ones
who belong at work, the men on TV
make a mess in Lucy's kitchen,
a pot of rice exploding
like a white volcano. The women
in the Philippines and elsewhere ponder
big business, the benefits
of discontinuing its own children. In dreams
these women package Toys "Я" Us uteruses
while a sterile Barbie, her hair tucked up
inside her Lucite helmet, plants
a flag for Mattel on the cheesiest moon.

ORIENTAL BARBIE

She could be from Japan, Hong Kong, China,
the Philippines, Vietnam, Thailand, or Korea.
The little girl who plays with her can decide.
The south, the north, a nebulous
province. It's all the same, according to Mattel, who says
this Barbie still has "round eyes,"
but "a smaller mouth and a smaller bust"
than her U.S. sister. Girls, like some grown men,
like variety, as long as it's pretty, as long
as there's long hair to play with.
On a late-night Manhattan Cable commercial,
one escort service sells Geishas to Go,
girls from "the Orient, where men are kings. . ."
White Ken lies on his stomach
while an Oriental Barbie walks on his back.
Or is it a real woman stepping on Ken?
Or Oriental Barbie stepping on a real man?
You have to travel to Japan
to buy this particular Barbie doll. A geisha girl
can be at the door of your New York apartment
in less than an hour. Of course,
there is no Oriental Ken.
Those who study the delicate balance
of American commerce and trade understand.

BLACK BARBIE HISTORY

Black Barbies look exactly like White Barbies.
Identical molds, not unlike uniform squares
of Nestles' Dark and Alpine White chocolate bars.
Even the Julia Barker doll, who was supposed
to resemble the actress Diahann Carroll, wound up
with White Barbie's tiny hands, flexed feet, and slight nose.
The star who played television's first single mom
was openly disappointed. But in 1967, Melba Moore gave her daughter
a "Colored Francie," claiming the Barbie doll
as a good role model for all girls, regardless of their race.
Barbie always keeps Mattel, her last name,
and she owns her own home and car. She always keeps
her trim figure, her waist not much thicker than her neck.
She smiles no matter what, never making herself
needy or vulnerable. Today, the same plastic surgery
used on Black Barbie can smooth those ethnic features
in all of us. We can all look the same, as we jump
into a vat of anesthesia and knives. So let's
bring our check books, our intolerable foibles, our fat selves.
There'll be no more competition when we emerge, identical
and redone, only dulled sisterhood and numbed love.

HISPANIC BARBIE

Born in 1980, she looks exactly like Black or White Barbie.
You can pretend she's Spanish, Mexican, Puerto Rican,
Columbian, Chilean, or Venezuelan. Shoppers
who complain she's hard to find should check Lamston's
or Woolworth's in certain neighborhoods of certain inner cities.

NATIVE AMERICAN BARBIE

There's only one of her left.

APOCALYPTIC BARBIE

Barbie didn't need air like the others.
Some of her sisters melted during the explosion,
but this Barbie had been tossed in a damp rumpus room
under a pile of moldy books. *I thought those missiles*
were destroyed, she heard the human husband scream
just before he burst into flames. *What about the treaty?*
cried the wife and the little girl. This was sad,
thought Barbie who felt unusually detached.
Maybe she was in shock. Maybe her emotions
were nuclear-tampered. She wished she could run
away from it all, and for the first time, her wish came true.
She pushed the books from her chest, stood up, and stretched.
An unlikely Phoenix rising from the ash, she rejoiced.
She had never moved on her own before.
She sped through the black streets, somehow
seeing. *There's not enough oxygen left to light a match,*
cursed a hearty cockroach who scampered beside her.
In the distance she could make out a slightly charred Ken.
They ran into each others arms, finally having the chance to live out
what was prior only in their imaginations. Barbie wished
for romance and a field of daisies or tall grasses.
Instead she heard hideous sirens, hinting
at further malfunctions. Barbie and Ken fled,
searching for a yellow sign—Fallout Shelter.
They hid behind sacks of flour and cans of baked beans,
hugging and fondling, without eggs or sperm,
without uterus or penis. Without tongues or breath, the two kissed
and vowed to protect each other forever. Without factories
or human children, Barbie and Ken were all each other had left.

SENSATIONAL BARBIE

"The Japanese have already perfected a lifelike geisha robot with artificial skin."

—Naomi Wolf, *The Beauty Myth*, 1991

When Barbie was under
anesthesia, her whole body
replaced with smooth plastic,
she swore she heard her doctors
telling smutty jokes.
When the surgeons sliced off her nipples
to put in the silicone implants
they decided to leave the milk-outlets off
because, after this, the nerve endings
would be dead and Barbie
wouldn't be able to feel
anything anyway. The sensation
in the rest of her breasts would be
diminished, but sexuality was not
why Barbie was doing this. She gladly
forewent her own pleasure for her race,
for womanhood, for survival.
Her clitoris and vulva's lips
were next to go. And her vagina
was sewn up, after the ovaries
were scooped out. Barbie couldn't
possibly give birth. After all
the expense her family went to,
she wouldn't insult her new body
with stretch marks. There were other women,

shorter and darker, who could carry Barbie's eggs.
That was their livelihood, up until
menopause. Some of these surrogates
told of dolls called Barbie they remembered
from their girlhoods and claimed
the elite women these days all looked remarkably like her.
The surrogates said there was a time when women
actually had their own names: Gloria, Andrea,
Betty, and Robin. The doctors
cut around Barbie's neck,
took off her head, and removed her
vocal chords and her brain. This
was when all memory was lost,
her youth, her adolescence, the smutty jokes.
And she was glad. How could
Sensational Lifesize Barbie bear it
any other way?

POWDER BLUSH

BLINDFOLDED BARBIE

No one was quite as fun at S&M.
Barbie smiled through the piercing,
the twisting, the teeth marks, the fire.
A magician swore he heard her laugh
when he sawed her body in half. Best of all,
there was no agreed upon password
to call the whole thing off.

KINKY

They decide to exchange heads.
Barbie squeezes the small opening under her chin
over Ken's bulging neck socket. His wide jaw line jostles
atop his girlfriend's body, loosely,
like one of those nodding novelty dogs
destined to gaze from the back windows of cars.
The two dolls chase each other around the orange Country Camper
unsure what they'll do when they're within touching distance.
Ken wants to feel Barbie's toes between his lips,
take off one of her legs and force his whole arm inside her.
With only the vaguest suggestion of genitals,
all the alluring qualities they possess as fashion dolls,
up until now, have done neither of them much good.
But suddenly Barbie is excited looking at her own body
under the weight of Ken's face. He is part circus freak,
part thwarted hermaphrodite. And she is imagining
she is somebody else—maybe somebody middle class and ordinary,
maybe another teenage model being caught in a scandal.

The night had begun with Barbie getting angry
at finding Ken's blow-up doll, folded and stuffed
under the couch. He was defensive and ashamed, especially about
not having the breath to inflate her. But after a round
of pretend-tears, Barbie and Ken vowed to try
to make their relationship work. With their good memories
as sustaining as good food, they listened to late-night radio
talk shows, one featuring Doctor Ruth. *When all else fails,*
just hold each other, the small sex therapist crooned.
Barbie and Ken, on cue, groped in the dark,

their interchangeable skin glowing, the color of Band-Aids.
Then, they let themselves go—soon Barbie was begging Ken
to try on her spandex miniskirt. She showed him how
to pivot as though he were on a runway. Ken begged
to tie Barbie onto his yellow surfboard and spin her
on the kitchen table until she grew dizzy. *Anything,*
anything, they both said to the other's requests,
their mirrored desires bubbling from the most unlikely places.

ASTROLOGY BARBIE

Barbie is a Pisces,
born during the last sign of the Zodiac.
Like others under the influence
of the wide seas, she's addicted to make-believe,
giving up childhood only when she absolutely has to.
When she was young, her astrologer told her that,
though she didn't desire money or fame,
Barbie'd have both someday. Advised that if she worked hard,
Barbie's potential for combining the material world
with her inspired philosophical vision
would be tremendous. The doll surrounded herself
with her birthstones: aquamarine,
ivory, and jade, and waited for romance.
According to the stars, she'd be drawn to those handicapped
in some way—a man in a wheelchair, maybe a partner
without a penis. When she met Ken, (a younger doll, by two years)—
born under the year of the Ox,
the second sign under the Chinese Zodiac—she knew
he would be tender, but never romantic.
Because she was a compatible Pig, a symbol
with kinder connotations in the East, Barbie
quickly got in touch with the authoritative
side of her nature. She decided that she and Ken
would be good mates, reading their horoscopes everyday,
their personality quirks rubbing against the cosmos.
Sometimes, they were chafed. Sometimes, it felt good.
Over pretend-tea, they often argued, good-naturedly,
about determinism versus free will. Sometimes
they were separated by children and tossed

into different toy chests. Other times, they lay
all night in one another's arms, true blue
as soul mates or Elvis Presley songs.

BICENTENNIAL BARBIE

Because she is the most popular doll
of the twentieth century, Barbie
is buried in a time capsule in Philadelphia
on July 4, 1976. She is scrunched between an empty Kentucky
Fried Chicken bucket and a full Coca-Cola can.
She's become a cultural icon, and now she has to pay
the price. She remembers a time
when just a few girls knew her
and she didn't have to put on such airs.
Now a full-fledged collectible, she has to make sure
every hair is always in place. I've just been voted
Best Personality, a superlative category
in our junior high yearbook. I'm able to pose
for a picture with the cute Best Personality boy,
the first and only football player
to ever ask me on a date.
He says he wants to go steady with me
and another girl at the same time.
I don't think it's fair,
but being the Best Personality girl,
it takes me a long time to say that.
You see, it's turned out that, though I'm too old
to still play with fashion dolls, they've somehow become
implanted in my subconscious. I don't look
anything like Barbie so maybe I don't deserve
a boyfriend of my own. And to make things worse, in my mind,
my rival resembles Barbie quite a bit.
When I finally write the Best Personality boy
an angry note, flustered, I slip it between the slots

of the wrong locker. The nobody boy who finds it
won't give it back, even when I ask him politely.
Soon everyone will know I'm not always in a good mood.
Fearing a scandal, I ask advice
of the Best Dressed and Most Likely to Succeed.
They say they don't care what the masses think—
and though I sense they're not telling me the truth—
suddenly it doesn't matter if my class
takes my Best Personality honor away or not.
At least I know I'm better off
than that one repressed Bicentennial Barbie
who'll be stuck in that stuffy time capsule
until the year 2076. Maybe
when she finally comes out, the pressure
will have been too much. Maybe she'll be able, like me,
to express herself. Maybe she'll wink at the Coca-Cola can
before they both shake, explode, make a mess.

BISEXUAL BARBIE

One of ten Barbies is left-handed,
another ten percent are lesbian.
But it's hard to keep track of the bisexual ones—
their orientation often secret, or if overt,
still undetectable. Barbies dress in front of one another
and statisticians think nothing of it.
Two Barbies often share a sleeping bag or double bed
because there are twice as many Barbies as Kens.
Two Barbies live in one Furnished Glamour Home
when each could easily afford her own.
When a Barbie closes her eyes, it's hard for her to tell
if she is reaching out to another Barbie or a Ken.
Female or male, the plastic doll-skin
is equally cool and smooth. Bald seamless crotches,
equally dry and unresponsive to touch. Both
have hard chests and legs that resist being spread.
The giveaway is always the hair—Ken's
is simply a splash of paint over his scalp.
But how many lonely Barbies—who've taken sophisticated trips
to Greece, New York City, and Italy—can be so straight
as to let a blond ponytail get in their way?

CODEPENDENT RELATIONSHIP

Barbie says to Ken:
You know what chlorine does to my hair.
But if you insist we go swimming
at least have the courtesy
to help me take my head off first.

PLANNING THE FANTASY WEDDING

"You're the only one for me," Barbie says, trying to bend
her arms enough to hug Ken. They're getting married
in only a month, and Barbie's confident she's made
the right choice. Because she's blond, she chose the dark
haired male fashion doll as her husband-to-be. Skipper
wants silk roses in her flower-girl bouquet, so Barbie
has to remember to call the florist to change her order.
The photographer is paid in installments, which is considerate,
but Barbie has to mark in her day book when to send in the checks.
She doesn't want Ken to throw her garter,
sure he will degrade all the women at the reception
in the process, but try to tell that to the deejay
who thinks the gesture is funny and cute. He insists
if Ken doesn't throw the garter, the guests will feel ripped off.
The bridesmaids' gowns finally fit the bridesmaids,
but now their shoes have to be dyed—and Barbie
has chosen a hard fantasy color, watermelon, that sometimes comes out
too light or too dark. The baker won't put the fresh flowers
on the cake unless they're arranged on a ring, so Barbie has to
      call the florist
again. Should the pew bows go on every other row?
Will they be too gaudy if there are too many?
Will Barbie and Ken look cheap if they skip? The premarital
counseling is next week, with the minister
who will ask them questions, trying to find their fundamental
differences, and remind them that married life is not
always a bed of roses. Barbie's gown has to be altered,
at the hem and the sleeves. It's at least three trips—
an initial fitting, a basting, then full stitches. The seamstress

has already had to cancel once because of problems with her ex-husband
which leaves a funny feeling in Barbie's stomach.
Barbie and Ken finally find traditional matching rings,
that aren't etched or brushed with a 90's mall look.
She makes her nail appointment for the day before the wedding
and the manicurist reminds her to be careful of her hands
between now and then. She has to get up at six
the day of the ceremony to have her hair curled into a bun and to starch
her veil so it poufs out enough. She had to hire
a second pianist because the first one didn't know all the music.
She has to call the honeymoon hotels and reserve rooms
with her Visa. She has to pick up the airline tickets
and find a good restaurant for the rehearsal dinner.
She and Ken had to look through the minister's prayer books
deciding the format of the mass. They weren't sure
whether to have communion, who of their guests would partake.
The replies come back so slowly, Barbie complains.
Her friends on the phone say they'll be there, but never
send their RSVPs. The friends who write they are coming
call back later to cancel with all kinds of excuses. Some want to
      let her know
at the last minute. Others say it depends on the price of air fare
or the health of their babies or cats. At breakfast,
Barbie finds herself snippy because of something
small that Ken says. As she times her hard boiled egg,
the pressure mounts. She cries out her wish—that all
she had left to do was to look good in a rented tux.

relates to poem on p.14

MARRIAGE

Barbie wonders if it's cheating

when she dreams of fashion doll boyfriends

Mattel never made for her to play with.

One with rastafarian dreadlocks—

spun with fuzz, not stiff

like the arcs of a plastic Jello mold.

Another chubby and balding

with John Lennon glasses.

And a third with a big sexy nose

like Gerard Depardieu.

Still, she supposes, Ken is harmless enough.

His pecs kept at bay by her stiff unyielding breasts.

And there's nothing he can force on her

when she's not in the mood.

She remembers discontinued Midge's last words:

"Hey, Barbie, it's a marriage, don't knock it."

From the stack of boys' toys across the aisle,

GI Joe occasionally gives Barbie the eye,

though he's not exactly what she has in mind.

In her box, elastic bands hold back her arms

and the plastic overlay she peers through

distorts her view of the world.

It's not only a romantic fling she desires:

there are hot air balloon rides,

night school classes, charity work.

Barbie comforts herself

knowing she's not much different

from the rest of us, juggling gratitude,

ambition, passivity, and guilt.

[handwritten annotations: "Mattle has dom. over her choice in boys. Shows how far the dom. Mattle has" / "Bob Marley" / "everything Ken isn't / all non-americas ; all artists" / "Superficial, everything she wants isn't, but can't have because it doesnt fit her script"]

TRAGEDY

—*for Kristin Pape*

Barbie grew dizzy like Belinda Palmer,
the actress who played Fay Dunaway's daughter
and sister in the film *Chinatown.*
Ken's stomach turned like Oedipus's did
when the Greek king realized Jocasta was not only his wife
but his mother.
>*Our faces have always been familiar*
to one another, confessed Barbie, *but don't all*
sweethearts say that?
>*Our bodies have such*
similar structure and skin tone, lamented Ken, *but being such narcissists,*
I guess that turned us on.
>So how were they to know,
introduced as potential lovers and wedding partners?
The mold of Ken's Mattel parts were labeled *Barbie's brother.*

MASCARA

WHY BARBIE AND KEN
DON'T DRESS IN UNDERWEAR

—for Sharon Stone

It is a complicated issue,
Barbie's signature trait of forgoing bra or panties,
whether she's out raking leaves or hostessing a formal party.
She rejects the tee shirt as an alternative
so this time it can't be solely political.
Ken wears his tux, unapologetically, without boxer shorts
underneath. Some speculate it has to do with titillation,
other's say it's because of their inadequate factory upbringing.
Without crotch moistness to ruin clothes, maybe the dolls
figure: *Underwear? What's the point?* Modest children
make do with Barbie's bikini and Ken's swimming trunks.
Modest adults prefer not to bring the matter up.

THE LIMITED EDITION PLATINUM BARBIE

Ever since Marilyn Monroe
bleached her hair so it would photograph better
under the lights, Bob Mackie
wanted to do the same for Barbie.
Now here she is, a real fashion illustration,
finally a model whose legs truly make up
more than half her height. The gown is white,
and the hair more silver than Christmas,
swept up in a high pouf of intricate twists.
Less demanding than Diana Ross
or Cher, Barbie has fewer flaws to hide.
No plastic surgery scars, no
temper tantrums when Mackie's bugle beads
don't hang just right. Calvin Klein
won't design certain styles
for any women larger than size eight.
He "doesn't do upholstery" is the way
he likes to put it. So imagine Bob Mackie's thrill
of picking up this wisp of a model,
Barbie weighing less than a quart of milk.
Imagine him dressing her himself.
The eight thousand hand-sewn sequins
which would have easily been eight million
if he had to design this gown for a bulky human.
Yes, Barbie is his favorite client—poised,
ladylike, complying. As he impales her
on her plastic display stand, Mackie's confident
she won't ruin any effect by bad posture.
Collectors can pay in four monthly installments

of $38.50 and have Barbie delivered to their home.
Others can go to Mackie's display at FAO Shwartz's,
the most expensive toy store in New York,
to remind themselves of who they'll never be,
of what they'll never have.

ANTICHRIST BARBIE

She could turn her head all the way around
like Linda Blair in *The Exorcist.*
Her bare high-heeled feet were begging to be nailed,
Jesus-style, to a cross. Mothers saw their daughters' dolls
levitate above pink carrying cases,
then tip upside down, arms straight out to their sides.
Barbie's an angel, cried the little girls who loved her,
who would mortgage their souls to be like her,
who would do anything she asked.

IT'S MY BODY

"There was a time when Barbie couldn't even
bend her knees," I tell my nieces Kerri and Katie
who sit before me on a living room floor
in blue and pink collar America.
They are strapping their Rock-n-Roll Barbies
into tiny leatherette pants
and big black guitars
with jagged lightning hips. Katie hands me
her doll because she needs help
with the teeny buttons that snake the back
of Barbie's off-the-shoulder blouse. "My first Barbie
couldn't even twist her waist." I am talking
like a person who has lived long enough
to see significant change. My nieces
have their backs to the TV which seems always on,
wherever I am. And behind their blond
innocent heads, Jessica Hahn
makes a cameo appearance on an MTV video.
She rolls like a sexy pinball,
then tries to claw herself out of a concave cage.
"It's my body," I recently heard her say
on a morning talk show. She started
by defending her nude poses in *Playboy*.
"It's my body," she repeated
like a Chatty Cathy doll
with a skipping record stuck in her back.
"It's my body," she began to answer
her interviewer's every inquiry—
where she grew up, if she still went to church.

"It's my body?"
The words stayed the same,
but as more accusations came, her inflections
changed. Jessica looked beyond the studio set
where someone seemed to be cueing her
that message. My lover was laughing.
"How about a little conviction there, Jessica?"
he said to the TV. Then, trying to coax
more conversation, he addressed me: "Look,
honey, she doesn't even seem to know if it's her body
or not." He was right,
but he knew as he brought it up,
it was the wrong thing to say.
I'd had too much coffee.
I found myself energetically defending Jessica,
blaming her disorientation
as a response to our misogynous society—
the dislocation all women feel
from their physical selves.
And then came the theories I'd been reading.
He left for work kind of agreeing
but also complaining that I'd made him exhausted.
And now my sister is blaming me for the same thing
because I am pointing out to Katie that she is mistaken
to think only boys should get dirty
and only girls should wear earrings.
"People should be able to do whatever they want."
I lecture her about my friend who wears a hard hat
when she goes to her job and works
with electricity, just like her daddy.
Katie fiddles with her shoelaces

and asks for juice. My sister says,
"Give the kid a break. She's only in kindergarten."
Older Kerri is concentrating, trying
to get a big comb for humans
through her doll's Moussed synthetic hair.
Because untangling the snarls needs so much force,
suddenly, accidentally, Barbie's head pops off,
and a smaller one, a faceless socket,
emerges from her neck. For an instant
we all—two sets of sisters, our ages
twenty years apart—share a small epiphany
about Mattel: this brainwashed piece of plastic cerebrum
is underneath who Barbie is. But soon
Kerri's face is all panic, like she will be punished.
The tears begin in the corners of her eyes.
I make a fast rescue attempt,
spearing Barbie's molded head
back on her body, her malleable features distorting
under my thumb. Although a grown doll,
the soft spot at the top of her skull
still hasn't closed. Under the pressure
of my touch, her face is squashed, someone
posing in a fun house mirror.
But the instant I let go, she snaps back
into a polite smile, her small perfect nose
erect and ready to make everything
right: Barbie is America's—
half victim, half little pink soldier.

BARBIE'S MOLESTER

His penis rises before him, a compulsion. He would take hormones if he could. In his best dreams he is natural, purposeful, like a rising moon. He begged his parole officer: *please don't let me out again.* But the psychological report showed he was ready enough.

His penis swells like a bump on the head and it hurts just as much as water on the knee. He's thrown away all his pornography and tries staying home as much as he can. He follows his counselor's advice: when the violence gets too much, he turns to another TV channel.

Things are tentative, though steady, until Christmas, when the Barbie commercials start to appear. He races to the toy store and yanks one of her from the shelf as hard as he can. When she doesn't struggle, he mistakes this for love. Suddenly he's doing things even he's never thought of.

BARBIE'S GYN APPOINTMENT

Her high arches defy the stirrups
and her legs refuse to open wide.
She has no complaints, cramps,
spottings, or flashes. It doesn't hurt
when the doctor presses on her abdomen.
There's nowhere for him to take a pap smear,
but Barbie's gynecologist suggests a D and C,
a hysterectomy, then a biopsy, just to be sure.
Barbie rebels as her breasts refuse to give
under the weight of the mammogram machine's plate.
She doesn't own a nightie suitable
for hospital wear, she explains, as she refuses operations
and scrunches the disposable examining frock
into a ball. She tosses it into the trash can
with relief. Not even Barbie looks good
in that pale green. She'll skip her follow-up appointment
on behalf of the rest of us who can't
and circle the globe, a tiny copy of *The New Our Bodies,*
Ourselves under her arm. The book will fire her imagination,
each chapter a fashion doll's version of the best science fiction.

BARBIE AND CARRIE

Barbie catches Carrie as a late-night movie. "Plug it up!" shout a group of mean teenagers while Sissy Spacek's character crouches in her high school's locker room shower. Carrie's mother, a religious fanatic, hasn't prepared her daughter for her first menses.

On her couch, Barbie hugs a bowl of make-believe popcorn. She thinks about how she doesn't ever bleed, even when she's cut. She's laughed politely at jokes about that nebulous time of the month, but knows nothing of cramps, mood swings, or bloating. She wears her white tennis shorts whenever she wants to and feels an absence of anything in particular when she gazes at the ever-changing moon. The only time Barbie used a sanitary napkin, it was as a makeshift mattress. She once held a junior size Tampax as a whiffle-ball bat. "Even Stephen King, who wrote the novel, and Brian DePalma, who made the film, understand the nature of female cycles better than I do, and they're human men."

Barbie's been told over and over again that she's been blessed with the best of adventures and fashion. But tonight she finds herself looking to dowdy Carrie as her heroine. Barbie knows nothing of telekinesis—she can't even will herself to move, never mind a pencil or ashtray. She watches the TV admiringly as Carrie takes her own life into her hands. And Barbie wishes she could experience the curse at least once.

BEATNIK BARBIE

Talk about failure.
Barbie couldn't snap.
Her fingers, venetian blinds
that refused to spread. Her thumb,
stiff and apart. No hep cat,
she had voluminous hair, too easily
flattened under stylish berets.
A face that could express so little
of the anger of her times. When she tried
to go barefoot, the balls of her tip-toed feet
grew tired and calloused. She liked the fringe,
the tie dye, and psychedelic posters.
Her friend Andy Warhol even did her portrait.
But she hadn't the veins for heroin,
the lungs for pot, the rhythm for jazz.
She preferred glamour to Ginsberg,
fashion to Ferlinghetti,
winsome beauty to William Burroughs.

HIPPIE BARBIE

Barbie couldn't grasp the concept
of free love. After all, she was born
into the world of capitalism
where nothing is free. And all she had
to choose from was a blond or dark-haired Ken
who looked exactly like Midge's boyfriend Alan.
Ken wouldn't even get bell-bottoms
or his first psychedelic pantsuit
until it was way too late, sometime in the mid-seventies.
And then, whenever Barbie tried to kiss him
his peel-off lamb-chop sideburns loosened
and stuck to her cheeks. There were no black male dolls yet
so she guessed a mixed-race love-child
was out of the question. Barbie walked her poodle
past the groovy chicks who showed their bellybuttons
and demonstrated against the war. She couldn't
make a peace sign with her stuck-together fingers.
She felt a little like Sandra Dee at a Janis Joplin concert.

LITERARY BARBIE

When Barbie reads Kafka's *The Metamorphosis,*
her whole body aches. She relates
to Gregor Samsa, the salesman-turned-bug,
who tries to explain his transformation
to his family, but who can only
produce tiny insect-squeaks. So many times
that kind of thing has happened to her.
Barbie's ouches gone unacknowledged, silent giggles
indicating appreciated tickles, lost shrill cries
for help. From the other room, she overhears a human
telling her friend that women make Barbie-feet
just before orgasm, pointing their bare toes to the edge
of the bed, even though they aren't wearing high heels.
Barbie has a thought, unsure whether it is
memory or pure imagination:

It's her, but not her,

under the stars, in a field of wet grass. She looks
like someone she doesn't know—a chubby girl
with problem skin and thick glasses. There is a hand,
her own or someone else's, between her legs
and she feels the beginnings of something
she's never felt before. In her terror of pleasure,
she whispers no to it all. And wakes up, immobile,
plastic, looking entirely like somebody else.

BARBIE AS MAFIOSA

—for Dangerous Diane

When she's slipped the bag of cocaine,
Barbie ducks into her favorite alley.
She pulls her head off and fills herself up
as though she's as innocent as a shapely salt shaker.
The wise guys leave the trafficking of small things to her—
and as she glides through international airports
or bustling loading docks, no one at the top's
disappointed. Whether nestled between the receiver
and base of a car phone, or tucked into a bedroom drawer
with a tiny tape recorder in her hollow torso,
Barbie loves fun and the thrill of adventure.
But being a no-nonsense doll, she can also give the kiss
of death if she has to. Her sassy lips
refuse to part, making her the perfect keeper of secrets.
At the press conferences, she'll deny all affiliations.
I'm just playing, she'll say, or
you can't prove a thing. I barely even have a brain.
When Barbie is this visible, sometimes
the big boss sweats. His wife gets jealous,
wondering why Barbie calls another woman's non-doll husband
from phone booths in the middle of the night.
The details of passwords, cement shoes, and unrefusable offers
all have to be worked out. The mob leader
will try to calm his spouse, claiming she's the only one
he loves: *This Barbie dame's not even a real dame.*
I don't know what you're so worried about.
The wife admits she feels silly, but when she returns
to bed, she keeps one eye open.

The cops feel silly, too, arresting toys,
so Barbie goes everywhere with the gall
of leaving her sunglasses at home. She frequents
the smoky private clubs and gets window tables
in Little Italy cafés. But it's the resort beaches
she likes best, where she can really unwind
and be herself. Her tiny cooler weighs down the corner
of her tiny designer towel. She watches her blond boyfriend
Malibu Ken fiddle with his flippers and goggles.
She loves him because he knows nothing—
a mere fashion accessory to Barbie's crimes.

MATH CLASS IS TOUGH
(1 October 1992)

Barbie hasn't spoken in twenty years
and when she finally does, little girls
and those who remember being little girls with her,
cock their ears, smile, and listen.
Math class is tough, says Teen Talk Barbie,
not quite exasperated, but certainly resigned.
Math class is tough?
Is that it?, we all wonder, pulling her string again
to see if she'll say anything more enlightening.
The American Association of University Women
wants Teen Talk Barbie pulled from the shelf
until Mattel agrees to let their favorite doll say something else.
There's enough anxiety around algebra, geometry,
calculus and trig. That's just what little girls don't need—
someone else telling them they'll never balance
a successful checkbook. Politicians
wonder if Barbie is Republican—
her soft analysis of math just in time
for the 1992 presidential election.
Is she being easy on Bush?
Math class is tough. . ..so give him a break,
why don't ya?, about the economy.
Imagine the White House's computer printouts—
full of indivisible fractions and prime numbers.
Barbie herself tried to run for president
against the Ross Perot Troll Doll, sure
her red white and blue cheerleader's skirt
would appeal to male voters. When she didn't

make the primary, tabloids spotted her
shopping at Macy's and eating a hot fudge sundae.
So maybe this time she's aligning with the feminists—
saying that math is particularly tough
on women—there are scales and dress sizes,
bust measurements and calories
all designed to keep us counting and counting.
Or in the United State's quint-centennial,
maybe she means that *math* is still *tough*
on Native Americans. Maybe Barbie
is rejecting our colonial commerce.
Little girls and scholars look for other metaphors—
Math could mean reason, logic. Class has the connotations
of socioeconomic levels—lower, middle,
and the wealthy. Tough could stand
for being resistant or stubborn.
In anagram-language *Math class is tough*
translates to *Last hog scum hat*
or *Shout at clam gist*. No one knows for sure
exactly what Barbie is talking about.
Yet we sense she picks her words
the way she picks her wardrobe—
nothing sloppy, always a grand design
that makes the rest of us feel half in, half left out.

MISS AMERICA 1990

Miss Arizona roller-skates to "Amazing Grace,"
and Miss Pennsylvania thanks God for her kidney transplant.
How lucky and right for them to be here—smiling, as they remind us
about unfortunate discrimination against the hearing impaired,
that it's so important for our youth to say no to drugs.
If we only recycled our bottles and cans, why
the world would be perfect, and they're here to prove it.
They're like cupcakes on a plate just for us,
like pheasants under the glass of our TV screens.
The "girls" have sliced off what they don't need—
extra fat on their noses, lumps jiggling
along their thighs. And they've pumped up
what they could use "just a tad" more of—
there's breast surgery and hairspray.
My friend Suzan-Lori says one of her first memories
in South Dakota was playing Playboy Bunny, strapping on ears
and hiking up her skirt. Who doesn't want to be desired? . . .
But she said she soon learned that no one could really love something
as flawless as Barbie. Her brother would unscrew
her dolls' heads, pull out their arms
by their tiny sockets, and bury the parts
separately throughout the yard. And when my friend Pammy grew up
in Brooklyn, she didn't need a brother to give her
a realistic sense of what she could expect.
Her Kens used to jump off the roof
of the pink Dream House and attack the Barbies
who'd be casually strolling by. While in Ohio,
Carole had parents who said, "No daughter of mine
shall play with a Ken," so instead she and her sister

improvised with Skipper—they wound tape around
her junior size breasts and cut off her hair
so she had to pose as a Casanova
with a short man's complex. And in Rhode Island,
kneeling under the Christmas tree,
I look up smiling, but as though in a confused plea—
in this photo I have my fist around the feet
of my first shapely doll and, in the other hand,
a box of Russel Stover's chocolates. Believing, even then,
in all kinds of answers, I took a pin
to my Barbie's permanently lipsticked lips
and carefully, with an eyedropper, fed her milk.
I thought I couldn't identify until she looked more like me.
But with nowhere to expel my good intentions,
she began to smell sour, and my mother noticed—
I had to throw her out. So until my birthday
and more presents, I only had Midge. My grandmother
made her tiny raglan dresses. The low-cut gowns
in the store—almost as expensive as the dolls themselves. . .
My grandmother taught me—who needed them?
But we did have to compromise—
if my doll wanted to wear shoes at all,
she still had to wear those treacherous heels,
Midge's feet permanently arched to tiptoe. . .
When my mother finally replaced my doll
it was with a dye-her-hair Barbie.
In one swoop of sponge and a waft of ammonia,
she could be a bright blond, a redhead, or a brunette.
It was fun. I was happy.
And needless to say, Barbie, like Miss America, never went gray.

EYE-SHADOW

BUDDHIST BARBIE

—for Nick

In the 5th century B.C.
an Indian philosopher Gautama
teaches "All is emptiness"
and "There is no self."
In the 20th century A.D.
Barbie agrees, but wonders how a man
with such a belly could pose,
smiling, and without a shirt.

BARBIE IN THERAPY

—for Becque

During the first visit, Dr. Midge asks Barbie to relax
and talk a little bit about her past.
But Barbie, the quintessential people-pleaser, doesn't know how
to do anything but smile. She's afraid
to tell Dr. Midge about the violence
of where she's come from: so many rolling heads
just like her own tumbling down a factory conveyor belt.
Her first pain was her hair being sewn
with a needle onto her bald scalp.
She never had time for any kind of childhood.
Not quite an orphan, yet not quite part of a family,
Barbie finds she's been given so little vocabulary
to talk about her feelings. *Try,* coaxes Dr. Midge,
tapping her pen on her pad. *I feel . . . frustrated,*
Barbie finally says, bursting into what would be sobs
if she possessed tear glands. *What do I wear*
to therapy? Barbie wants to know. Dr. Midge
recognizes her client's question as avoidance,
but answers anyway believing in not pushing too fast.
Sweatpants are good, Dr. Midge says, *or anything loose*
so you can feel comfortable lying on the couch.
Dr. Midge asks Barbie to draw a picture of herself
to use as a springboard, something for them to talk about.
Barbie renders herself perfectly, just as she appears
on the packaging she comes in. Dr. Midge is thrown—
She's used to having anorectics draw themselves as blobs,
or the heavier women scratching out little stick figures.
You are quite an artist, Dr. Midge praises, double-checking

68

to see if Barbie has included all her limbs.

I have a little pallet at home, Barbie says.

It came with an easel, smock, and beret.

Really? asks Dr. Midge, interested. Barbie answers, dejected,

Yes, but there's no real paint, so what's the point?

That must make you angry, coaxes Dr. Midge.

No real food in your fridge. No real hay

for your palomino's western stable.

Barbie asks her shrink to explain what anger is,

and Dr. Midge suggests several good books.

She gives Barbie therapy-homework, asking her to punch

her pillows every night before she goes to bed.

Barbie writes out her first check, hoping

that just around the corner, she'll get to the real issues

which are full and fleshy, and anything but plastic.

what are they?
Maybe find her human characteristics

THE PHILOSOPHY OF LONGEVITY,
ACCORDING TO BARBIE

Barbie fills out the application for the job.
Tammy, her owner, is not there to tell her
that an employer has no right to ask
her height and weight. Twenty eight centimeters,
approximately two ounces.
On her own, Barbie has enough political awareness
to flinch as she fills in her measurements:
16, 8, 16 and wonders if she should convert
from metric to inches. She, of course, could quite easily—
Barbie is very good at math.

To stand out from the others who want the position,
she attaches her powder pink resumé
that's about the size of a postage stamp.
Barbie wants to work for the airlines,
see the places that have inspired her outfits.
Personnel thinks she'll be perfect.
Her perpetual smile is but a solid painted white line.
No twenty eight individual teeth to rot and dig
into the funds of their dental plan.
Thirty two, counting wisdom!

Barbie would correct them
if she were able to make noise.
The boss curses the bulimics he's hired in the past
and how much money treating their gingivitis
has drained from the company.
Like most people, he makes the mistake

of thinking Barbie can't hear him.
Her little primitive ears, commas without the swirls
indicating some inner workings. Just one of those details
that make her seem less than human:

the white polka dots over her eyes
that suggest her pupils shine
regardless of the direction of light.
Her hair sewn on in rows that end abruptly,
and wisp-less, at the nape of her neck.
I want nipples, she's often longed to say.
And fingers that can separate from each other.
I dream of dexterity and crying.
But Mattel will never let her talk—
they know Barbie's seen too much.

There were spurts when she thought real change was coming.
Her 1965 bob, when she was finally able
to cut her hair. Then, in 1975,
when the U.S. Federal Judges ruled that girls
should have the same access
to school sports programs
as boys. Or 1984—when she was 25
and wearing tuxedos. Old enough to vote
for Geraldine Ferraro, Barbie thought,
I just can't stay plastic forever!

But before she knew it, she was again in party dresses,
and in a backlash a few years later—
the world apprehensive about the actual way women smell—
a lavender-scented Barbie hit the toy stores. . .

As soon as her boss shows Barbie her flying schedule,
she realizes there are so many other things
she still wants to do. She longs
to write short stories. She's never climbed
Mount Everest. When she comes home, and kicks off
her pumps, Tammy senses Barbie's disappointment.

She tells her doll, *Getting what you want*
is usually that way. Tammy isn't jealous
of Barbie's optimistic veneer and good girl-next-door looks.
She knows inside Barbie's pain is real.
She often defends her doll to her hissing friends:
Don't you know that if Barbie suddenly came to life
she would only be five foot seven?
She couldn't even get a real modeling job.
That's why she always wears heels.
And her waist would be close

to what the Guinness Book of World Records reports
as the smallest of all time.
Barbie's no simple Pinocchio.
She has severe body image problems.
As Tammy makes her case on the phone, Barbie
lies on her stiff canopy bed and silently considers something
even more complex. What, Barbie thinks,
if I am already dead? She sees no future
of her own, not a single line
on her molded palm. Suddenly her furniture

is all tiny coffins. Each couch looks plush
on the outside but, in fact, is hard and uncomfortable.
She begins to write furiously in her Cracker Jack diary.

She laments that Tammy and she are the same age,
but look how much Tammy has done—
how many words she's spoken,
how many dress sizes she's grown through!
People remember Barbie the way they remember the deceased:
the last time they saw them. *A person dead*
at fifty will always be fifty, Barbie thinks.

But what about me? She wants to scream,
Doesn't anyone see I'm growing older!
Her miniscule temples begin to bulge.
Tammy hangs up the phone, barely noticing
her doll's distress, and says,
You and me, sister, we've got a lot in common.
She means that they're both single women over thirty.
Both own way too many clothes.
And rarely does a straight guy ask either of them out.
Maybe Tammy is laughing

because she is in denial of her own hurt.
But Barbie, feeling more alone than ever, passes out
and while unconscious, has an archetypical
fashion doll nightmare. She is in a garbage heap,
and her persistent body is one of the slowest things in the universe
to disintegrate. Tammy, Raggedy Ann, and all the books
Barbie loved are already recycled
back into earth and rain. She sees herself left
and reproduced by the millions
in varying degrees of disarray and decay:

dirty bathing suits and torn taffeta gowns.
Missing limbs and matted hair.
She wants to run away, but can't.
It's the same dream-sensation of being stuck
that her owner so very often has.
Tammy picks up Barbie whose eyes,
if human, would flutter. *I think of you as family,*
Tammy says as she kisses her doll's forehead.
The artificial skin feels feverish to her lips,
but Tammy thinks it's because of the sun streaming in.

Barbie's sticky-with-caramel diary falls from her hand.
Since Barbie can't eat anything,
her owner has always given her the prizes.
What are you up to now, girl? Tammy kids.
She's unable to decipher the teeny chicken scratch
that makes up Barbie's hysterical entry.
She returns her doll to her special shelf,
thinking that's where she likes it best, and sighs,
I know I've got to let you go,
but I'll sure miss you when you learn to fly.

HOLOCAUST BARBIE

Barbie was born after World War II,
in the midst of its consequences—disgruntled women
back in their United States' kitchens. Barbie'd
only heard of the over-sea's atrocities, but was more certain
she was reincarnated with each horror story, with each little pang
of her deja-vu. Her Aryan air, the ease in
which her arm, unable to bend at the elbow,
would salute. The terror when she saw a pile
of dolls like herself, naked and dirty, in the mass grave of a toy chest.
Barbie sought hypnotists and healers,
who all saw the connection, though none could be sure
whether in her past Barbie was the Nazi or the Jew.

MORMON BARBIE

When she takes the tour in Salt Lake City,
the Mormon missionaries point out
that the marble pillars in the Tabernacle
are really cleverly painted wood.
It is then that Barbie feels right at home,
her own mansions often full of faux decorations.
But it is the idea of having her own planet
in the afterlife that hooks her—so she signs up
for her free gift, the Book of Mormon,
and begins her conversion. She is told
she can baptize the dead, rescue the fallen Barbies
who might by now be somewhere in hell
or just regular cloudy heaven. She visits the Genealogical Center
plugging the words Barbie and Mattel into the computer.
Her family extends in every direction,
the huge globe full of Barbies just like her,
who all need to be saved. She performs
as many absentee baptisms as she can,
but tires more easily than usual, now that she isn't allowed
caffeine. Like other Mormons, she starts getting high
on sweets and sharing Ken with other women
to conserve her energy flow. She begins to sew
high-collared dresses and melts down her feet
so that she can finally wear loafers.
She has operation after operation
in hopes that she can have many Mormon children.
With Donny and Marie Osmond music in her Walkman,
she strolls Salt Lake City's divinely-inspired ten-acre blocks.
She reads up on Brigham Young and quotes the Bible

in ways to suit her. She prays for Mattel

who constantly tries to get her back

with empty promises of sequins and a line of plastic infants.

Sometimes one of Barbie's earthly days seems forever,

her personalized pink planet swirling high above the world

      as she knows it.

She dreams of her Maker, the Lord Jesus Christ,

and Ken who will, in the afterlife, call out her secret marriage name

so she will fly to him, no longer Barbie,

no longer misunderstood at every turn.

SISTER BARBIE

After years of promoting glitzy consumerism,
Barbie decides to repent.
She wants to make a radical offer,
give her entire life up to God.
With the trepidation of the prodigal son,
she knocks on a convent door
seeking guidance. But, to her surprise,
the toy companies have beaten Barbie to the idea.
A foot tall play-nun answers.
Her habit is sewn up tight,
and her sleeves are hemmed directly onto her plastic hands.
A plastic face just like Barbie's is glued over her wimple.
The kindly Sister explains that if this indeed
is Barbie's calling, she will never be able to go naked again.
She demonstrates that she and her distinctive dress
are all one piece. Barbie asks about the play-nun's eye shadow,
and they both conclude it must have been the factory's mistake.
A human starts the cassette tape of hymns
that's included with the Cozy Cloister.
A voice begins side one
telling the child who's bought Sister Barbie
that a percentage of the cost will go to charity.
Then the play-nun proceeds with a tour of the place.
There are hard benches and cheaply made statues.
Barbie recognizes the relics of play-saints
as cloth remnants from her old, less successful, outfits.
Father Ken in his polyester vestment silently passes,
a priest-collar painted directly onto his neck.
There are rosary beads, and an empty jar

labeled Holy Water. The little girl
who takes care of the play-nun
has also made communion wafers with a paper hole puncher.
A muzak version of "How Great Thou Art"
blasts through the house. A human mother from down the hall
yells, "Turn those holy songs down, goddamn it!"
A cardboard lamb bleats.
A crucifix topples down from the cloister wall.
Even her "roughing it" Country Camper was made better,
Barbie notes. Gothic velveteen curtains
would spruce things up. What about a gold tabernacle?
The play-nun patiently clarifies the vows of poverty.
Secular Barbie likes Sister Barbie a lot.
So when she thinks about the shabby nunnery,
her self-blame compounds.
She's already beginning to have serious second thoughts.

BARBIE IN THERAPY, PART II

—for Becque

Barbie is starting to become dependent
on Dr. Midge's every word. The patient asks her doctor:
*What should I do about exercise? Run in place each morning
or jump on my personal trampoline?* In conversation
with other Barbies, she often starts sentences
with *My therapist says.* . . The other dolls notice
she has a certain glow that she hadn't had before,
but Barbie's sisters aren't crazy
about all her changes. She's begun, every once in a while,
to say no, not wanting to share her fantasy clothes
because of something called boundaries. Barbie's past comes back
to her in flashes, like mini-deaths:
little boys poking their sticky fingers
between her legs; pet dogs gnawing on her hands.
And just how is she supposed to feel about Ken?
Sometimes he's a soda jerk, a book worm, a mere bowling partner.
Then other times she's thrust next to him—he in a tux,
she in a wedding dress. He lies on top of her,
but nothing happens. The children watch Ken fail
to get an erection. When they laugh, her brother/husband/doll
blames Barbie, saying it's because she won't loosen up.
Dr. Midge proposes Barbie might suffer from vaginismus
and the M.S.W. confesses to having the condition herself.
Barbie, thinking Ken is too much trouble,
begins to dream about Doctor Midge, their bodies
rubbing together like two plastic pieces of kindling wood.
Awake, Barbie longs to put her head in Dr. Midge's lap
and has to fan herself when she spends too much time

dwelling on this. Because her shrink's body
is so like her own, [Barbie wonders if desiring Dr. Midge
is simply a desire for herself.] The pamphlets
about masturbation remain unopened in Barbie's top drawer—
her curiosity about the mysteries of penises barely there.
Barbie thinks maybe she is ready to join the ranks
of other famous women—Jodie Foster, Dolly Parton,
Whitney Houston—who will spend their careers
keeping their secret from fans.
But Dr. Midge tells Barbie not to worry,
her attraction may be transference, that many clients get crushes
on their M.S.Ws. As Dr. Midge (the red-headed version
of her client) clears her throat, Barbie claims, flirtatiously,
she's not worried at all. Until now,
the only true love either doll has ever known
has come from the hands of little girls. Barbie tenderly counts
Dr. Midge's freckles, as though each one contained an answer,
as though together the micro-beauty marks were aware
of the infinite moons and stars that they really were.

is Barbie's problem that she is in ♡ w/ herself.

- lives for Dr. Midge
/through her before it was for Mattel

-

Barbie can't find help is it tragic

Dr Midge is so similar to Barbie, only dif. is that Midge has red hair & a degree.

BARBIE JOINS A TWELVE STEP PROGRAM

Barbie is *bottoming out,*
she's sitting on the *pity pot.* She hasn't the know-how to express
any of her emotions. Before she even gets
to her first meeting, she takes the first step, admits
her life *has become unmanageable.*
She's been kidnapped by boys
and tortured with pins. She's been left
for months at a time between scratchy couch cushions
with cracker crumbs, pens, and loose change.
She can't help herself from being a fashion doll.
She is the ultimate victim.

She humbly sits on a folding chair
in a damp church basement. The cigarette smoke
clouds the faces around her, the smell of bad coffee
permeates the air. The group booms the serenity prayer:
God, grant me serenity to accept the things I cannot change,
courage to change the things I can, and wisdom
to know the difference. Poor Barbie is lost
in a philosophical quandary. Her God must be Mattel.
How can she *turn her life and will over* to a toy company?
Must she accept her primary form of locomotion
being the fists of young careless humans?

And what can she change? The only reason Barbie
is at the meeting at all is because she wound up in the tote bag
of a busy mother. She toppled out when the woman,
putting on lipstick at the bathroom mirror, spilled the contents

of her bag onto the floor. The mother didn't see Barbie skid under
   a stall door
where a confused drunk, at the meeting for warmth,
was peeing. *Never thought Barbie had problems,*
she said, picking up the doll. She thought it would be funny
to prop Barbie in the last row. No one else noticed the doll
as she fidgeted in her seat. The hungry drunk
went on to spoon a cupful of sugar into her coffee.

Barbie sat through the meeting, wondering:
What is wisdom? What is letting go?
She wished she could clap like the others
when there was a good story about recovery. She accepted
she couldn't, hoping that if she stopped struggling,
her higher power, Mattel, would finally let her move.
Miracles don't happen overnight, said a speaker.
Take the action and leave the rest to God, said another.
Barbie's prayer that she would be at the next meeting was answered.
A member of the clean-up committee squished her between the seat
and back of the folding chair and stacked her, with the others,
   against the wall.

BARBIE AS RELIGIOUS FANATIC

—for Becque

Eve, being one of the first born
ever, had no bellybutton because she'd sprung
from no womb. Barbie thinks how her birth, too,
was sterile and bloodless. Aligning herself with the holy,
she says proudly, *I will never miss the comfort of a uterus.*
I will never know a faulty mother.
But raised in a society that does its best
to trample female spirit, Barbie had also been taught
to feel bad about what she lacked. As hollow
as the Tin Man, she was ashamed
about her absent heart. She thought herself inadequate,
emptied of bones or bowels. So it was also the unfulfilled nature
of this doll that readied her for religion. Before the fall,
Eve, like Barbie, had no period, no cramps, no pain
in childbirth. And now Barbie's friend Judy,
The Mommy-To-Be-Doll, similarly makes delivery a snap.
No stretch marks or screaming, no afterbirth or drugs.
Judy's stomach is a trap door that hides a clean infant
with a full head of hair. Take out the child, press her belly down,
and Judy can immediately fit into Barbie's clothes.
Barbie wonders if her friend is a sign:
Could Judy be a virgin though she has no vagina?
Could the immaculate conception be applied to plastic?
These tiny child-saviors, both White and Afro-American
like their mothers, could easily fit in the cribs
of decorative mangers in holiday homes.
Could the world's next messiah be a girl?
Could Barbie's friend Judy be the next Mary?

Although no biblical scholar,
Barbie is smart enough to put two and two together.
She knows she arrived years before Ken, without the help
of any of his ribs, which makes her wonder
about Adam, if he really did beat Eve
to the garden of Eden. Barbie pictures herself, an apostle
to the initial wave of the second coming
as she collects her religious pamphlets—
the *Good News, Smile—God Loves You,* the ones
given out by the Jehovah's Witnesses. She crosses out
what she doesn't believe and sprinkles the text
with arrows and Judy's name. Shoppers gather
as Barbie preaches her version of religion at the corner
of the Toys "Я" Us doll aisle. The wars
and natural disasters go on, surely, just
as Barbie predicts. Though the smaller children believe her,
at first they are too busy playing
to see her connections. Some heathen kids toss
Judy's baby daughter in the bottoms of their toy chests
to leave her there for years. Barbie says, *Doesn't anybody see?*
She puts on her bikini and points to where her bellybutton should be.
Her voice is sheer will, without the aid of battery
or pull string. And Mattel, Barbie claims, as her loving God.
She's especially successful in the conversion of girls
as they grow older and see their flaws. They praise
Barbie's paradise—her clothes, her homes, her cars.
She's as free as they ever hope to be—
with no toy-apples anywhere in sight.

BARBIE'S FINAL TRIP TO THERAPY

There's nothing wrong with me!
There's something wrong with society!
Barbie screams, gutturally, the way human babies do
when they're hungry. Over the months, her voice
has grown from tinny to raspy,
tentative to commanding, deepening every time Dr. Midge comments
about Barbie's newest breakthrough.
Barbie has learned that depression is nothing
but anger turned inward, so now, as she lashes
out towards the world, she giggles, too,
because the expulsion of energy feels so good.
If she were a lazier doll, Barbie would wait
for the world to change. Because
she is so well-preserved, she'd still look the same
one hundred, even two hundred years from now—
if that's how long it takes to get the E.R.A. passed, *equal rights amn.*
if that's how long it takes for women to be safe on the streets.
But afraid those days for her kind will never come
when the results of her activism seem slow or null,
Barbie wishes she could immediately skip over to the afterlife—
hoping Mattel's manufactured her a toy-soul that isn't sold
separately. Never really having felt full-fledged suicidal,
Barbie talks about this longing with her therapist
on her last visit. Dr. Midge is reassuring—
all great thinkers ponder what will happen after death.
Dr. Midge is confident Barbie is ready to strike
out on her own and recaps her patient's psychological accomplishments
and growth, the doctor saying she's learned quite a lot
about herself as well. With a firm handshake, the two dolls try

to say goodbye at the end of the hour, then fall

into each other's less professional hugs.

Barbie will miss her shrink, but Dr. Midge, preparing

her client for separation, has taught her

to also include other women in her life.

Barbie's begun hanging out with Lisa Sliwa,

the national director of the Guardian Angels.

The two will be interviewed for magazines, proposing all men

who rape should be castrated. Barbie is sick

of taking cabs at night, of double-locking the back door

to her Furnished Glamour Home before she ascends the spiral

staircase to her bedroom. She knows more women

go to see therapists than men, that more women

have been locked up in looney bins,

so a combination of history and current events

prompts her to smash her three thimble-size saucepans.

After her final therapy session, she crushes

her tea kettle that never learned how to whistle

with the pointed heel of her pump. She tosses

the toaster out of the picture window

of her Sweet Roses Living Room. Then, out

with the tasteless make-believe toast. Her poodle

and daisy apron, her MBA briefcase,

her Oscar De La Renta dresses. Sick of posing

as anything but herself, she's even tired

of the oversized shirts she's borrowed from Ken.

That same night, she takes a midnight jog, past her lawn

which looks as though it's been set up

as a garage sale of fashion accessories. She's naked

as the first day she was made in the factory,

as naked as Eve, as Lady Godiva, as naked as Jane

[handwritten annotations: "script change(?)", "trad. feminen objects", "throws out Mattels identities", "endless possibilities"]

when she took off her animal skins
to escape the jungle and her bad marriage with Tarzan.
Barbie is as vulnerable as Cinderella
in that split second between her dissolving rags
and the instant gown her Fairy God Mother bestowed her.

Maybe she hasn't changed.

Therapy Poems are about:
- finding yourself, but not liking
the end result
- transformation to More human
traits
-

AFTERLIFE BARBIE

Upon first entering Heaven and the World of Angels, little spirits
are given Afterlife Barbies, brighter than any film or TV
versions of cottony good-deed-ghosts. In the Hereafter, Barbies
don't possess telltale big boobs or teeny accent-mark-feet.
Instead, they resemble white flashlights enveloped in dry ice.
And Afterlife dolls have no separately purchased coordinating outfits,
but come with a series of statuette-humans
and animal-figurines. The practicing seraphs try rescuing:
tots on tricycles speeding down driveways
into traffic; anesthetized women on operating tables;
rabbits squirming in hunters' traps.
And for intermediate celestial beings—
townsfolk falling through cracks of a toy-earth
made by a fake intensity-ten quake.
The newly-dead all appear as identical twins—
swirly balls of light, male and female spirits curvaceous
in the same way. Only how bright their shine
distinguishes angels from one another—the more daring
their recoveries, the higher intensity of their glow.
The recently-transformed look to the Afterlife Barbies
as role models, and what the dolls radiate
is what students of archangelship aspire to also.
The newly-dead are glad at first—no more
body image problems, ever, they think. Yet the dolls
gleam in a way that is beyond otherworldly,
beyond neon, beyond God's sun. Soon the interning cherubs
feel inadequate, that no kind feat is ever enough.
They see their luminous reflections as dull, doubt
that they belong in Paradise at all. No one traces this malaise

to Afterlife Barbie, her beatific blankness,
her commandments living in synthetic animation.